GRIMMY Co

TM

**Starring Mother
Goose & Grimm
by MIKE PETERS
Introduction by
June Lockhart**

TOPPER BOOKS

AN IMPRINT OF PHAROS BOOKS • A SCRIPPS HOWARD COMPANY

NEW YORK

Library of Congress Catalog Card Number: 90-061719

Pharos ISBN: 0-88687-508-0

Printed in the United States of America

Topper Books
An Imprint of Pharos Books
A Scripps Howard Company
200 Park Avenue
New York, NY 10166

Pharos Books are available at special discounts on bulk purchases for
sales promotions, premiums, fundraising or educational use. For details,
contact the Special Sales Department, Pharos Books, 200 Park Avenue,
New York, NY 10166. (212) 692-3976.

Dear Grimmy,

Good luck in your newest venture. With this book, "Grimmy Come Home," your career expands to other media.

You will undoubtedly make feature films soon, and following the release of the movie "Grimmy Come Home," there will, of course, be "Son of Grimmy," "Courage of Grimmy" and "Grimmy's Great Adventure" to mention only a few in a lengthy list of box-office hits.

Then will begin the successful TV series called simply "Grimmy." It will be a great triumph for you, and will run for years and years.

And, if I'm very *very* lucky, I'll get to play the mother part.

Bravo, my darlin' Grimmy! Go for it!

Love,

June Lockhart

June Lockhart

To a wonderful young cartoonist,
Todd Williams,
as a symbol of all unrealized potential

NO PAIN, NO GAIN...

THUD

CHASING CARS IS GREAT EXERCISE...

"...ANYBODY'S CAR."

4-12

I LOVE RIDING IN A CAR...

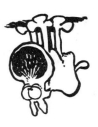

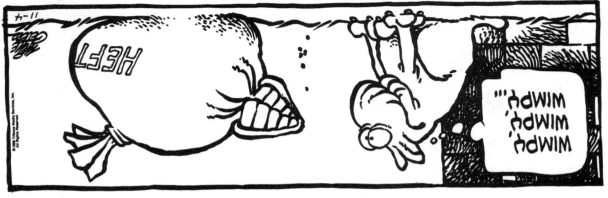

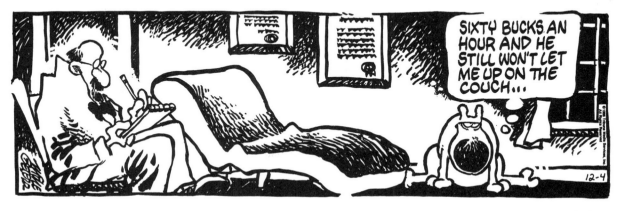

CREAM AND SUGAR?

OK. "YOU TRY BURYING A BONE IN JANUARY."

RAT TAT TAT TAT TAT TAT TAT

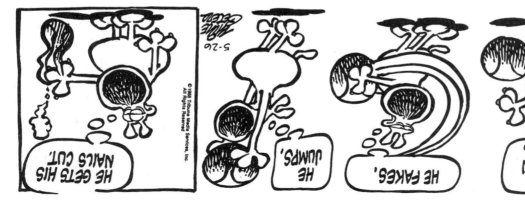

MAYBE THAT CUTE POODLE
WOULD LIKE ME IF I USED
SOME UNDER-ARM SPRAY,

WHICH ONES ARE
MY ARMS ?...

DOGS LOVE BOUNCING ON BEDS...

BONK BONK WHHHIRRLL WHHHIRRRLL

5-21

DOGS HATE CEILING FANS, HOWEVER.

LOOK AT ME... THERE'S GOT TO BE MORE OUT OF LIFE THAN JUST CHASING CARS...

AND EATING DISGUSTING GARBAGE OUT OF TRASH CANS.

5-23

NAAAAAAAAA

BEEP
BEEP
BEEP

POLICE

I'M WEARING A FUZZ BUSTER.

6-13

WHO SAID YOU CAN'T JUDGE A BOOK BY ITS COVER?

6-18

"I ALWAYS WAVE AT THE WEATHER SATELLITE..."

"HI..." "HI, EVERYBODY, HI..." "HI..."

"OH, BOY...THERE I AM ON T.V."

"THIS ONE SMELLS LIKE A TELEPHONE BOOK..."

SCRATCH SCRATCH

"I LOVE SCRATCH-AND-SMELL BOOKS..."

GRIMM... YOU'VE BEEN DIGGING IN MY GARDEN TOO LONG.

GRIMMY, WHAT DID THE MAILMAN BRING US TODAY?

MACE.

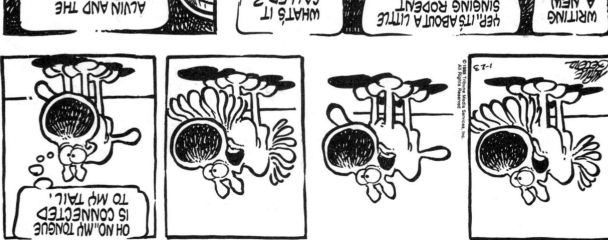

GENTLEMEN, START YOUR ENGINES.

PRRRRRRRRRRR RRR

SNIF SNIF SNIF...

YOURS ↑

MINE ↓

FAIRY DOG MOTHER

OK, MY CHILD, YOU MAY GO TO THE DUMPSTER, BUT YOU MUST BE HOME BY MIDNIGHT.

THAT'S THE LAST TIME I CHASE A RENT-A-WRECK.

GOSH...THIS SAYS PLUTONIUM HAS A HALF-LIFE OF TEN THOUSAND YEARS.

I WONDER IF ANYTHING ELSE LASTS THAT LONG?

CHEESE WHIZ.

2/5

OH, OH...LASSIE IS REALLY IN TROUBLE THIS TIME.

HIS SPONSOR HAS DROPPED HIM BECAUSE THE RATINGS ARE DOWN...

AND NOW THE NETWORK MAY CANCEL HIS PROGRAM...

BOY THESE SHOWS ARE GETTING REALISTIC.

3-3

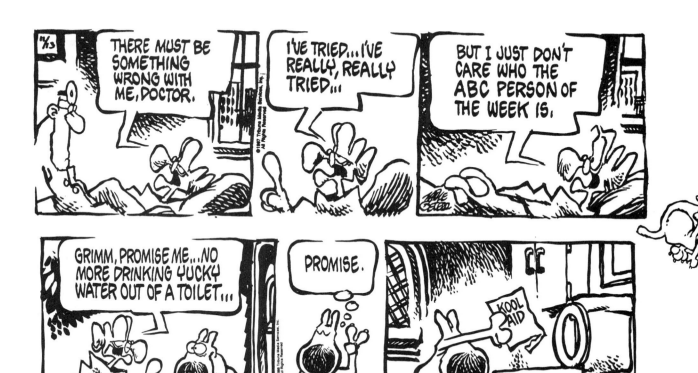

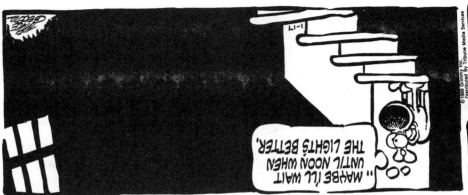

QUICK, FIND SOMEPLACE TO HIDE...THE BATHROOM! THAT'S IT..THE BATHROOM.

NO BLOODTHIRSTY PSYCHOPATH WOULD EVER THINK OF LOOKING FOR SOMEONE IN A SHOWER...

1-23

OOOH...MYYY GAAWWWD..

WHY DID I STAY UP AND WATCH "NIGHTMARE ON ELM ST."?

1-24

NOW I'M AFRAID TO TURN OFF TV AND WALK UP-STAIRS TO BED IN THE DARK.

MAYBE I'LL JUST SLEEP HERE ON THE COUCH.

TV IS THE NIGHT LIGHT OF THE '80'S.

SNIF
SNIF

ATTILA

GRAB

ATTILA

JUST WHEN YOU THOUGHT IT WAS SAFE TO GO IN THE LITTER BOX

ATTILA

1-27

IT'S SCARY WHEN YOU'RE ALL BY YOURSELF IN THE DARK.

CREEK

SNAP

AND THE HOUSE IS FULL OF ALL DIFFERENT KINDS OF WEIRD NOISES,

BUMP THUD

SNAP

AND THEN YOU REALIZE...

POP

BONK

...MOST OF THE NOISES ARE COMING FROM YOU,

CREEK

SNAP
POP

1-28

Heeeeeeeeeeeeeeeere's GRIMMY™

Now you can order all three MOTHER GOOSE & GRIMM books!

✂ -

Please send me

_____ copies of STEEL-BELTED GRIMM
at **$5.95** each

_____ copies of 4-WHEEL GRIMMY at
$5.95 each

_____ copies of GRIMMY COME HOME
at **$6.95** each

_____ TOTAL BOOKS (Please add .50
per book for postage and
handling)

My check for $ _____ is enclosed.

Ship to

NAME _____

ADDRESS _____

_____

CITY _____ STATE _____ ZIP _____

Make check payable to PHAROS BOOKS. Send order to:
Sales Dept., Pharos Books, 200 Park Ave., NYC, NY 10166.
Please allow 4-6 weeks for delivery.